ON FREUD'S PSYCHO-ANALYTIC METHOD AND ITS EVOLUTION.*

BY JAMES J. PUTNAM, M.D.,

Professor of Neurology, Harvard Medical School.

THE subject of psycho-analysis, on which your long-honored president has invited me to speak, is one that deals with serious and difficult problems. I shall be glad if I can throw a flashlight on them here and there, and in so doing I shall try to answer some of the questions which have most frequently been asked me concerning the subjects in hand. Do not suppose that I shall pretend to give directions such as could enable any physician to put this method into practice. On the contrary, I beg you to regard it as a matter for congratulation that the leaders in this movement have a strong sense of the need of careful training and high standards on the part of those who desire to join their ranks. I have recently returned from a trip abroad, where I made the personal acquaintance of quite a number of the more prominent psycho-analysts, attended their congress and was able to learn a great deal about the details of their mode of work. I came away strongly impressed with the fact of the recognition on their part of the importance of their task and that this recognition had had a good effect on the mental attitude of the workers, many of whom are still young and full of promise.

These men seemed to me, for the most part, strikingly eager, earnest and sincere. " Sie haben gelernt ein Stück Wahrheit zu ertragen," said Freud to some of us when these facts were under comment. I learned to my surprise and interest that the greater number of the investigators had subjected themselves, more or less systematically, to the same sort of searching character-analysis to which their patients were being subjected at their hands. It is fast getting to be felt that an initiation of this sort is an almost indispensable condition of good work; and for this important reason: The main thesis of the supporters of these new doctrines, — which are at bottom old doctrines, rearranged and re-emphasized, for psycho-analysis is largely an accentuated

---

* Address before the Harvey Society of New York, November, 1911.

phase of education, — is that most of the emotional disorders to which we give the name of psychoneuroses arise largely from an instinctive self-concealment, and concealment of one's self from others; that is, from an unwillingness or an inability to see or look at all the facts that should be seen, respecting one's own tendencies and motives, as the basis for the control of feeling, thought and action. Recognizing this principle, these physicians have seen that so long as their own lives, too, are partially on a false basis, so long as they also are self-concealed, they cannot do justice to their patients, either in the way of appreciation or of criticism. Obviously, a person ridden by prejudices that he does not recognize cannot do justice to another person in a like state; one is reminded of the simile of the " beam " and the " mote." It is, therefore, I repeat, a matter for congratulation that the need of preparation for these tasks is being taken seriously, and the assertion is justifiable that the introduction of this specialty is likely to make better men, in every sense, as well of the physicians who practice it as of the patients whom they treat.

But while no man, however able, can without long study master the details of this method, every man who would be liberal or scientific can and should master its principles and give the movement his generous sympathy and support.

What is psycho-analysis, and what, in general, are its aims? Psycho-analysis is a method of investigating and treating nervous invalidism and (incidentally) faults of character, which owes its strength to the fact that it searches and studies in detail, so far as this is practicable, all the significant experiences through which the patient to be treated has passed, and the motives and impulses which have animated him at psychologically important moments of his life, even since his earliest childhood. In doing this it discovers, not, indeed, all the causes of the disorder from which he suffers, but a large number of important partial causes, and thus prepares the way for the influences tending toward recovery. This definition is, I think, substantially correct, but it needs some explanation, amplification and qualification.

First, it is not strictly true to say that the attempt is made, during a psycho-analytic treatment, to pass in review all of the important motives and impulses, or even all of the kinds of motives and impulses, which had animated the mind of the person who subjects himself to this treatment, but, strictly speaking, only a

On Freud's Psychoanalytic Method And Its Evolution

James Jackson Putnam

In the interest of creating a more extensive selection of rare historical book reprints, we have chosen to reproduce this title even though it may possibly have occasional imperfections such as missing and blurred pages, missing text, poor pictures, markings, dark backgrounds and other reproduction issues beyond our control. Because this work is culturally important, we have made it available as a part of our commitment to protecting, preserving and promoting the world's literature. Thank you for your understanding.

certain class of them, — those, namely, that were originally based on emotions which had been repressed because they were painful or seemed out of harmony with the chosen plan of life, but which, in spite of all repression, had remained as active causes of serious mischief. It does not systematically deal with those motives and impulses which may be designated as aspirations and ideals, derived, as I believe, from the essential endowment of the spiritual nature by which every man is animated and which is to be regarded as an independent, primary, creative force. Psycho-analysis does not, in other words, pretend to take the place of philosophic teaching; but it does help, even without claiming to do so, to give such teaching a better chance to make itself effective.

On the other hand, it is not just to characterize psycho-analysis solely as a therapeutic measure. In proportion as the psycho-analytic movement has developed toward maturity, it has shown itself able to make scientific contributions of great value to psychiatry,[1] psychology, mythology, philology, sociology, as well as to education and to prophylaxis. In other words, these investigations bring support to every research which deals with the inward and the outward manifestations of human effort and mental evolution, while at the same time they draw important aid from all these inquiries into the psychology of the human race, for the benefit of the single human life.

The practical aim of this method is to enable persons who are hampered by nervous symptoms and faults of character to make themselves more efficient members of society, by teaching them to shake themselves free from the subtle web of delusive, misleading, half-unconscious ideas and feelings by which they are bound and blinded as if through the influence of an evil spell. Such persons — and in some measure the statement is true of all persons — have to learn that they are responsible, not only for the visible, but also for the hidden portions of themselves, and that, hard as the task may be, they should learn to know themselves thoroughly in this sense. For it is the whole of ourselves that acts, and we are responsible for the supervision of the unseen as well as for the obvious factors that are at work. The moon may be only half illuminated and half visible, but the invisible half goes

---

[1] The value of Jung's argument for ranging Kräpelin's dementia precox, together with many symptom-complexes classified by Janet as psychasthenia, under the psychological category of the introversions, is now generally conceded.

on, none the less, exerting its full share of influence on the motion of the tides and earth.[1]

Some patients may learn to override or sidetrack their troubles and can be helped by various means to do so. These other means are, however, not to be compared, for power of accomplishment or permanency of result, with that of which I now speak to you.

It is difficult to see why any broad-minded person should refuse to recognize, on theoretic grounds at least, the value of the self-knowledge here alluded to, especially when the treatment of the more serious forms of psychoneurotic illnesses is at stake. These more serious forms are very numerous and the causes of enormous suffering. Difficult and doubtful of issue as the treatment of them is, the method here discussed holds out a new hope of great promise.

It would obviously be impossible to offer you anything approaching to an adequate account of the means by which it is sought to discover, for each individual case, the particular facts and tendencies from which the particular symptoms that are present may have sprung. It must be enough to assert the fact which Freud established, that each person's memory, if allowed and encouraged to wander, uninhibited by resistances and repressions, may usually be counted upon to furnish the information that is needed. Where this is insufficient, two other plans may be adopted, one of which, indeed, comes largely into play in every case. These two methods are, first, the use of word-associations, the value of which Dr. Jung, of Zurich, has done so much to establish, and, next, the study of dreams.

The significance of the word-association method, stated in briefest terms, is that it serves as a sort of concentrated conversation. The patient, answering at random as he should do, instinctively lets go, for the time being, of the reins which he ordinarily holds tight over his inmost thoughts, and allows glimpses into the mental processes which it is of the utmost importance that he should know yet which constantly tend to elude his attempt to seize them. Further inquiries and associations may, then, if necessary, proceed from such beginnings.

The elucidation of the means by which the interpretation of dreams may be successfully carried on, and a path thereby opened into the inner chambers of the mental life, is one of Freud's contributions which well deserves being designated as a mark of genius. Whatever differences there may be between the conscious lives of different individuals, in our repressed and unconscious lives we are all very much alike — not, indeed, in detail, but as regards the principles in accordance with which we are constructed.

Just as we speak the same verbal language, so we speak, at bottom, the same dream language, and can learn to make the meaning of our dreams clear to others and to ourselves. It cannot be too often represented that the disharmony between the conscious and the unconscious portions of our lives, which is sometimes productive of so much misery, ought not to exist. Every one recognizes this after a fashion, and tries, instinctively, but, as a rule, without success, to overcome the disharmony by finding some sort of outlet for the repressed — and usually childish — feelings which his conscious intelligence will not tolerate. But this is not enough. If he would really overcome the disharmony, he must meet the situation face to face, and the study of his dreams, in which his repressed thoughts are represented in caricature and in picture language, is perhaps the best means of obtaining clues to the information which he seeks.

These hidden portions of our lives must be thought of as seeking to make themselves felt in action though not in words. Ordinarily, we keep them, like the evil spirits in Pandora's box, under pretty strong lock and key. At night, however, the locks are loosened, and our repressed emotions succeed in finding their way to the theater-stage of consciousness. Even then, the thoughts which arise are not allowed to become too evident, but are concealed beneath picturesque symbolisms and disguises.

It is a very interesting fact that, as each new person comes into the world and begins his life of dreams, he adopts forms of symbolism analogous to those which have been in use since even semi-civilized life began. The various animals with which our childhood was familiar come forward to play the rôle of animal-passions; the rapidly moving trains typify our hurrying emotions. And so, too, still or moving water, the rooms or buildings in which we like to place ourselves, the bare or varied landscapes, and many a symbol more, are all utilized as elements of a picture-language which is almost as well defined as that indicated by the rebuses of the child, or the hieroglyphs of the Egyptians, or the mythology of the ancient Greeks.

So full of meaning are these signs that no dream carries its true, much less its whole, significance on its face; no item, no obvious omission even, is without its bearing; hardly a feature or character is to be found that is not of even multiple value. The general proposition has been laid down — and certainly with good reason — that every dream represents the fulfillment of an unconscious wish. No one would doubt that this statement is true of the day-dreams of childhood, and when for " wishes " we read " partial " or " temporary " wishes, and learn by self-study what these partial wishes are, it is found in the dreams which appear so terrifying, the wish is concealed behind an attempt to repress it, just as the partial wishes of our waking moments are often concealed behind the disguise of fears, a phenomenon very characteristic of the phobias of neurotic patients. Persons unfamiliar with the interpretation of dreams often deny this tendency, and point out that their dreams are nothing but jumbled representations of some trivial happenings of the day before. It is true that every dream takes the happenings of the day before as materials out of which to construct its apparent story. These trivial experiences are utilizable, partly because of their analogical bearings, partly because they are still conveniently available by the memory and yet not fully woven into any other of the various complexes of which our emotions tend to weave themselves. In utilizing these experiences the dreamer does what any person might do who wished to tell a story while sitting at the dinner-table with his friends. Assuming that he desired to describe a journey he had taken, he might select a salt-cellar to stand for a castle that he had seen, a fork for one road, a spoon for another road, a plate for a pond or lake, etc. But behind these hastily chosen symbols, there would be a connected story; and in the same way, behind the trivial details which make the outward framework of the dream there is a connected story, which, indeed, reaches, in layer after layer, back into the dreamer's earlier life and even into his childhood. For in every mental act the whole personality of the individual comes into play, although in each act certain elements of the personality are illustrated far more than all the rest. Of course, it need hardly be said that the analogy between the forks and spoons and the apparently trivial incidents of the day previous to the dream-night is by no means a complete one. Unimportant as the real incidents may seem, they are often full of meaning, which, however, only an expert analysis can reveal. Each dream, then, furnishes, to the expert, and to the patient, a path into the inmost recesses of the patient's life, better than any other means could furnish.

As regards the therapeutic value of the psycho-analytic method, it is almost needless to say that there are many cases that baffle every treatment, not excepting that by psycho-analysis, and that this method has its special limitations. The patient, to be treated with success, must be reasonably young, reasonably intelligent, and able to give a large amount of continuous time to the investigation. His outlook as regards conditions of life must be reasonably favorable, or else he must have the capacity for idealization such as will enable him to override outward misfortunes, and to face existing conditions cheerfully. He must want to get well, and not count on his illness as giving him gratifications or advantages which he is unwilling to sacrifice, even for better health. Then, of course, some sorts of symptoms are less curable than others.

The length of time sometimes required for successful treatments has often been the subject of comment. But in fact it is a great gain to have a method capable, even in a long time, of producing fairly good results. Any one who thinks about the matter must realize that it is extremely difficult to make any considerable change in one's own character or habits. Our good qualities, as well as our faults, are deeply founded. Both have their roots in the experiences of infancy or in the reactions of childhood, and if we would help ourselves to the best purpose we must get back, in knowledge, feeling and imagination, to the conditions under which the deviations from the normal first began. To accomplish this takes time and patience, though the task is full of interest.

It would not be justifiable to assert that the psycho-analytic treatment can accomplish such results as are claimed for it if we could not assert at the same time that the investigations based on psycho-analytic studies have thrown new and important light on the *nature of the disorders* with which the method deals. Without this light, a rational, causal treatment of these affections would be as far out of our reach to-day as it was in the last century, and we should still be throwing ourselves against the rocks and reefs of this great problem, chipping off a bit of stone here and there, but making no consistent progress.

The splendid insights of Charcot, and the remarkable researches of Pierre Janet with regard to the phenomena of automatism and the mental state of hysterical patients, brought the first real illumination into this obscurity, — an obscurity greater than we then could realize. The lines on which Freud began to work were somewhat parallel to Janet's in that both of these great leaders quickly learned to recognize the importance of the apparently forgotten and seemingly dead experiences of the invalid, and showed that they might still be acting as motive forces in the affairs of the present moment. Freud soon arrived, however, at the important conclusion that it is not enough to know single incidents of the past life, let them be never so grave, but that the whole life must be drawn upon and made to yield its entire history, and he proved that when the whole life is exhaustively studied on this plan it is possible to explain the symptoms of illness as largely referable to demonstrable influences operating since birth, and thus to get on without making such large drafts on "inherited tendencies," of which we know so little, as the principal causal factor. Then it gradually became clearer that the gaze of the investigator must be directed with ever greater insistence towards the very earliest years of life as the time when the seeds of mischief are sown, — that marvelous period when tendencies are established and paths of least resistance are laid down, which may give a set or bias to all the years to come, and cause the child's mind to become sensitized, as if through a process of anaphylaxis, to special influences which may be brought to bear later, though perhaps not strongly until a much later period. The life-history of the normal child became, naturally, the next object of these ever-widening studies, and then the attention of a special group of investigators was turned upon the childhood-history of the races of men, as described in sagas and in myths. Even the history of criminology and of sexual perversion, — already mapped out in part through the studies of many men, but now for the first time made to yield its true lessons, — has been largely drawn upon, for the sake of discovering and illustrating the nature of the dangers with which the early years of every child are more or less beset.

One instructive method of getting an idea of what passes in the child's mind, of the difficulties which he encounters and the means that he takes to meet them, is to observe carefully how we ourselves deal with corresponding situations: Every one who is accustomed to scrutinize his own thoughts and conduct must realize that he is often tempted to put out of sight what he does not like to think of; to seek enjoyment instead of doing work, and, in general terms, to live on a mental plane lower than his best.

Most of the temptations by which we are beset might be classified under one or the other of two headings; namely, the desire for gratifications or undue self-indulgences of a relatively personal sort, and the desire for gratifications implying the approbation, admiration or the attention of others, if only through subserviency or domination. I am not now concerned to prove the prevalence of these temptations or to deny that we may utilize them to our profit, but only to call attention to the fact that a more or less universal and sometimes irresistible tendency exists, which impels us, on the one hand, to secure these gratifications, and, on the other hand, to protect ourselves from self-reproach for so doing. In the interest of these two motives, which are, of course, comparatively rarely conscious motives, we cloak our cravings under forms which tend to make them seem justifiable and even admirable.

Every thoughtful person is more or less aware, — though it is only the well-trained or unusually discriminating observer who can thoroughly appreciate the fact, — that an element of craving for self-gratification may lie hidden under the guise of anger, prejudice, fear, jealousy, depression, desire for self-destruction, "over-conscientiousness," and the wish to inflict or to suffer pain. It is equally true that under the form of restlessness, or that of a sense of incompetency, we symbolize the hidden conflicts which cover our desire to escape from ourselves, or our incapacity to understand or unwillingness to face the full meaning of our emotional desires.

Those of us who call ourselves " well " owe it to those who are forced to call themselves " sick " to study the true nature of these innumerable faults of character. When this is done, it is discovered that these faults deserve the name of "symptoms," and that, like symptoms, they are disguises and compromises, concealing painful conflicts that may date back to the experiences of infancy.

It must be remembered that between the period of birth and the later years of childhood each individual recapitulates in a measure the history of civilization. The parent and the community who see in the infant not so much what he is as the promise to what he is to be, make little of those qualities in him which would be considered as intolerable if judged by our adult standards.

But these qualities exist, nevertheless, and the growing child to whom they are transmitted must deal with them as he is best able, whether by gradually modifying them for the better, or by shrinking from them in disgust, or by continuing to indulge himself in them in concealed forms. One fact must never be forgotten, namely, that each child comes into the world with one mission which he cannot overlook or delegate and which he shares in common with every living thing, — the mission of preparing to do his part in the perpetuation of his race. For the sake of the establishment of the great function on which this depends, he is provided, in infancy, with a considerable number of capacities in the way of sense-gratification and with ample means of indulging them, which, however, he must eliminate as he grows older or preserve at his risk. But this risk the infant does not see, and before the time comes when he can see it he may have found himself drawn into paths of least resistance, leading both to pleasure and to pain, from which it will be difficult for him to escape. There is, then, no easy course left open for him but to repress his desires for these indulgences, just so far as may be necessary for concealing them from himself, while at the same time he invents substitutes and compromises in which the indulgences are continued under a new form. Yet, unfortunately, the adoption of such compromises is equivalent to laying a foundation for defects of character or for symptoms of obstinate forms of nervous illness, as the case may be.

Clear memories of these earliest years of childhood rarely are retained. Yet some individuals retain very much more than others, and this fact, taken in connection with the evidence furnished by dreams, by a few careful observations of young children, and by the memories of patients trained under the psycho-analytic treatment, leads to the conclusion that a large part of the apparent forgetting is based really on repression.

From the standpoint of the next later period many of the details of infancy are unpleasant to recall. One is reminded of the Mohammedan cadi who, when asked about the early (Christian) history of his town, replied: "'God only knows the amount of dirt and confusion that the infidels may have eaten before the coming of the sword of Islam. It were unprofitable for us to inquire into it."[2]

[2] Cited in James's "Psychology," vol. ii.

The period of childhood, though it contains many elements of happiness, which are usually accentuated and continued by the child's delightful power of grief-compensating fancy as exhibited in day-dreams, contains also many elements of suffering. The child's fears — of the dark, of storms, of mystery and power in a thousand forms — have been explained [3] as due to the organic memories of his pre-human ancestry; to the recognition of the contrast between his weakness and the bigness and strength of those about him or (in a religious and philosophic sense) the vastness of his own inexhaustible possibilities. There is nothing to urge against these explanations, but they cannot be regarded as covering the ground. The young child is at least partly like the older child and the adult, and fear, with them, cannot be studied as apart from the desire which so often underlies it. Like Scott's aged harper, we all "wish, yet fear," and frequently the wish becomes gradually repressed, and the fear alone remains. We all "fear" those most whose approbation we most "wish," and fear the tests in which we most long to succeed. The child, with his splendid fancy and his intensified training in the symbolism of fairy-tales, loves to play with these fears and wishes. The dark stands for delicious, as well as alarming, mysteries, and beyond these there is almost always the longed-for chance of the pleasure of re-discovering himself in his mother's arms.[4]

The strength of the child's tendency to follow pleasurable paths of least resistance may be vastly diminished, or, on the other hand, vastly increased, by the fact that the immense forces of social custom, by prescribing what should be done, help to deprive the child of his own sense of responsibility, while at the same time they seem to relieve the parent from the necessity of seeking to discover what is really passing in the child's mind. We talk of independence, but, in fact, the community is almost fanatic in its demand for conformity. The key to the solution of these difficulties must be sought, not primarily in the education of the younger generation, but in that of the older. It is with the lack of knowledge on the part of the parents, and the disregard by physicians of the need of acquiring and imparting adequate information on these subjects, that the reform must deal. There can be no doubt but that our social and ethical customs, which

---

[3] *Cf.* Pres. G. Stanley Hall's paper: Study of Fears. Am. Jour. Psychol., January, 1897, vol. viii, pp. 147-249.
[4] This pleasure has a philosophic bearing to which I cannot here allude.

represent the filtered experience and wisdom of the race, are of immense value. But the ends which they mainly seek and the methods which they follow are not chosen with reference to the needs of the neurotic child. These points are of such importance that an attempt must be made to state them somewhat more fully, even at the risk of exciting misunderstandings.

The family influences under which most healthy-minded children grow up are, of course, eminently beneficial, and this is no place for discussing their shortcomings.

But the fact remains that nervous invalidism is extremely common; that it is closely bound up with social relationships of varied sorts; and that the school in which the child gets his first introduction to these relationships is the home.

One cause of unhappiness in married life, for example, is the inability on the part of the husband or the wife to adopt the new duties with a whole heart. This inhibition is often due, in part, to the craving, established in childhood, for an undue continuance of the parental ties, with all that they imply; an unconquerable homesickness, which often cannot be put into words or recognized in its own form, overrules the new interests which ought to be supreme.

These are facts of common knowledge, but under the light of this new movement they have been studied with a thoroughness previously impossible, and have been correlated with others of a kindred sort, with the result of immensely increasing their significance.

It should not be forgotten that father and mother are not only objects of admiration, imitation and veneration to the growing child, but that they stand likewise to him as man and woman, and that, as such, they are in a position of peculiar responsibility and may be centers of peculiar harm.

I am not undertaking here to lay down rules for conduct, nor even to assert that although, on the whole, frankness and a well-guarded, thoroughly wholesome intimacy between parents and children is eminently desirable, it is very undesirable to break down all barriers of restraint between them. The evolution of modesty and of a certain amount of personal reserve needs to be safeguarded, even at some risk.

Real knowledge with respect to these complex matters should be sought, but it is hard to get and its advent is not to be awaited with impatience, or its acquisition as the basis of judgment and conduct assumed on insufficient grounds.

Another point of importance is that the dawning self-consciousness of the infant represents him to himself, not definitely and distinctively as " boy " or " girl," but as a being standing in relations of dependence to other and more powerful beings, whose characteristics he does not classify from the sex-standpoint. The significance of this statement will be understood without difficulty by any one who will consult carefully even his own experience and observation. Every one must be aware that we all have some traits which are commonly designated as masculine, and others designated as feminine, and that the evolution which best marks social progress is based on the working out, in the case of each person, of capacities related to both of these sorts of traits. The attraction which persons of our own sex have for us is of great value as leading to friendships which may become exceedingly warm without ceasing to be eminently desirable. It is, however, well-known that such friendships may develop into relationships which are eminently undesirable and a-social, and even, in the case of men, of a kind that would be called criminal. Between these two extremes, tendencies are to be observed, or are to be detected through careful study in a given case, which may lead to hidden conflicts and to distressing nervous symptoms. Good observers have shown it to be true that just as, to a certain degree, many men prefer the society of their fellows at the club to that of their wives and families at home, so, in a much deeper sense, nervous invalids often waver between attractions which would lead them in the direction of the most wholesome and useful relationships, either of marriage or friendship, and those which have an unwholesome tendency. The objectionable forms of these tendencies, if not created, are, at least, accentuated, by the over-strong, or, rather, by the slightly abnormal attachment of the infant to the father on the one hand or to the mother on the other. It is true, at the same time, that there are probably also deeper influences at work, dependent on some tendency which each person brings into the world, but of the exact nature of these latter influences it would be premature to speak. The subtlety of the danger here noted is what gives it its effective power, for what could seem to be freer from danger than parental love? Obviously nothing, when this love is fortified by wisdom and knowledge. In fact, however, it happens but too often that, either because the child is too immature in his manifestations of affection or because the parents retain too much of their own childishness, that which should be a source of infinite happiness and should lead the child towards independence and self-reliance becomes, instead, an opportunity for the growth of unwise emotion and a weakening tendency to imitation and dependence.

A careful study of the child's personal gratifications has shown that a portion of the earliest and strongest of them, which, for the most part, have to be repressed later, are related, first, to the satisfying of hunger, then to the securing of certain specific pleasures, such as the massive feelings of warm contact (during the diaper period), and those due to the excitation of the orifices of the body, especially the mouth, the urethra and the anus. To the child these sources of gratification stand at first, both morally and from the social standpoint, on an equal footing. He is unaware that he is likely to be subjected to serious temptations with reference to some of them; he does not know that his reaction to them may decide whether he is to become a being capable of recognizing that his best freedom is to be found in a willingness to devote himself to the welfare of the social whole, or whether self-indulgence is to be his ruling motive. The child who continues too long to suck his thumb, or wet his bed, or who finds undue fascination in the emptying of the bladder and the rectum, or detects a mysterious significance in these events, may be acquiring a tendency to prolong bodily indulgences which ought to be outgrown, and laying the foundations for other personal gratifications of more subtle, more distinctively mental, and, socially, of more disastrous sorts. Masturbation, of course, although accused of dangers which do not belong to it, stands high among these over-indulgences of a purely personal, auto-erotic sort.

Freud has been criticised for making too much of the sexual element in these problems; for seeing sexuality where it does not exist. But is this criticism just? The number of those who think so is growing daily less, as sober judgment and knowledge of the facts come better into play. Think with what inconceivable, with what seemingly unwarrantable tenacity, nature, bent on the perpetuation of the life, both of the individual and the race, has safeguarded the function on which this depends. Many plants if starving will flower all the more abundantly, as if in order that their descendants at least may live. Think how every novel, every drama, is founded on some aspect of the sex problem. Is not the truth rather that these problems are felt to be of such enormous importance that we ought perhaps to shrink from touching them just as we might shrink from handling bombs charged with dynamite of high explosive power? And yet, is this true? Is not the dynamite to a great extent the figment of our imaginations, filled with repressed memories which we have not known how to study, but whose rumblings we have all vaguely felt within us?

This, or something like it, was, at any rate, the feeling which led Professor Freud long ago to enlist for his campaign, and determined him to risk everything for the laying bare of these long-neglected facts. He might have said to himself, whether he did or not, that he would take the great studies of human character, like those by George Eliot or by Meredith, and would go on where these writers stopped, striving, in the spirit of the novelist turned man of science, to discover the processes of childhood through which the strong, deep tendencies which they describe came into being. Those who oppose this movement out of unwillingness to discuss the sexual life are not only declining to be scientific and impartial (since to the scientific person nothing is in itself disgusting or unworthy of consideration), but also are rendering it harder for patients to get well, by stamping as indecent their attempts to gain a true knowledge of themselves.

I should like to call your attention to the fact that in the beginning it may be only a slight over-accentuation of an infantile tendency that makes the difference between the promise of health and the promise of invalidism. But when the lines which enclose the angle of deviation have become extended, as the child grows up to manhood, the actual distance becomes immense. One is reminded, here, of Jean Ingelow's poem, "Divided," and, still more, of George Eliot's great study of Tito, in "Romola." Charming, handsome, kindly, scholarly, Tito seemed, as a youth, to have all possible good qualities, save that he possessed, or was possessed by, an apparently trifling tendency to self-indulgence, or selfishness, of the concealed, insistent, infantile type. This was never very prominent, but it was always present and always irresistible, and it made him in the end a fiend. And yet, from the psychoanalytic standpoint, Tito's was a curable case. At any moment, up to the very last, if he could have been aided to penetrate the history of his own life, and thereby to see at one glance the system of interlocking forces representing his still active tendencies of childhood and their logical outcome in his present acts, — as one looks through a transparent model of the brain-tracts, — he might perhaps have undone the mischief. For a man's emotional and mental past, even if of his infancy, never dies; it is always present and active, and represents a force which is always susceptible, theoretically at least, of modification or neutralization, in the interest of progress.[5]

There are several advantages in classifying, as Freud has been criticised for doing, the many and varied tendencies of which novelists write, as sex-tendencies. But perhaps the most important advantage is the practical one that it enables the physician, on suitable occasions, to point out the direction in which a given act or thought, conceivably innocent in itself, may lead.

It would be worth while to know whether, when you lay your hand on a man's shoulder, you are to be taken for a friend or arrested for assault and battery. The strongest term which points to the possible practical outcome of your act is oftentimes the best. A bit of self-indulgence, if it represents a force which had its rise in infancy, may not be as harmless as it seems. The child must, at every cross-road, select and accentuate on the one hand, repress on the other. But this power of selection and repression, which stands so high among our attributes, is itself a source of danger. The adoption of this or that *principle* of accentuation or repression may become habitual, and some of them are harmful. The child is like a merchant who cannot oversee all his affairs in detail and so indicates to his subordinates the general trend of his policy and then lets them work it out alone. But let him look out lest he become narrow-visioned and get hoodwinked. The really wise merchant does not often leave his subordinates to work out his plans indefinitely by themselves, whereas the indication of policy made in early childhood is often a decision, in one or another particular, made once for all and for a lifetime. Truly, the child is the father, — indeed, the master, — of the man, to a degree hard to appreciate except for those who have taken the great

---

[5] Strictly speaking, we never obliterate the memories of our past experiences, and even to wish to do so would be in accord with the spirit of an Oriental rather than of a Christian philosophy. The new growth to which we should aspire diverges at a certain point from the old but gains a certain richness from the memories of the latter, and these memories cease to be painful, in the old sense at least.

amount of pains required for following the literature of these researches of which I speak to-night.⁶ Not only is the policy of the lifetime often dictated once for all in childhood, but this fact itself is often erased from memory, that is, it is repressed, and the results of an early misjudgment are then accepted as if assumed to be governed by an intellegence cognizant of facts and tendencies of which in reality it knows nothing.

To summarize once more what I have said: Nervous invalidism, in the sense in which I now mean that term, is not only a source of suffering: it is also a sign that those who suffer from it cling, — unwittingly but under the pressure of strong instincts, — to modes of thought and feeling which should be recognized as belonging to childish stages of development. The mode of action of this tendency is subtle, but a crude illustration of the principle indicated is given in the obvious fact that depression and feelings of weakness and incapacity, painful though they are, are often made to serve as self-indulgent and childish self-excuses from effort, and as means of exciting self-pity and the attention from others which almost all children so much crave. The simple recognition of this tendency is, however, not competent to banish it from the mental life of the adult; the whole chain of experiences and shifting emotions which led to the habit must be laid bare and scrutinized. It is, then, found that men sometimes allow themselves even to fall sick, or to suffer pain, or to adopt some species of asceticism or of morbid self-depreciation, for the reason that behind these symptoms and tendencies there lurks often a desire for self-gratification of a childish type the real root of which can usually be revealed in detail, and must be revealed if a radical cure is to be obtained. In the case of neurotic phobias, it is, essentially, himself, not the supposed source of terror, that the patient mainly fears. So, too, morbid introspection is largely a search for emotional excitement, the desire for which only disappears when its true nature is clearly exhibited by the aid of a deep-going introspection of a totally different, a more wholesome and more rational sort, through which we see ourselves, no longer as unfortunate individuals, but as companions in arms in the great march of social progress; as akin, perhaps, with those whom we had called sinners, and had pitied at long range, but akin also with men of devotion

⁶ It would be obviously impossible even to indicate here the mischances which often come with the later years of childhood, when curiosity and fantasy become active; still less those which attend the oncoming and course of adolescence.

and force, whose characteristics we can discover to have been won by conflicts like our own.

Broadly speaking, it may be said that every man has had, theoretically, at his birth, the capacity of developing, under favorable conditions, in such a way that he could have become possessed of a fairly well-balanced character, and that this capacity was the best element of his birthright. The conditions required for this development may have been such as it would have been extremely hard, even impossible, to secure at the outset, but in the psycho-analytic method we have a means of readjustment, difficult of application, it is true, but through the aid of which at least a certain number of those who have gone seriously astray may be restored to reasonable health. But for this purpose they must teach themselves to review their adolescence, their childhood, and their infancy, and thereby to strip off the veils by means of which their ease and pleasure-seeking instincts had sought to conceal them from themselves.

The game is worth the candle, for, in my estimation, no disease with which men suffer causes, in the aggregate, so much misery as the fears, the obsessions, the compulsions, the needless weaknesses, the innumerable faults and vices of character, by which we see ourselves surrounded. All these ills spring virtually from three sources, — inherited tendencies, the failure duly to recognize our spiritual origin and destiny and the obligations which this recognition should impose on us, and the absence, during our development, of the conditions necessary for the successful making of the journey from infancy to adult life.

It is very important to note that the infant starts on his journey of life with a series of instincts, motives and inhibitions which are less strongly unified than are those of the adult. He does not at once feel the intense repression and directive force of public opinion which is to be reflected later by his mother and his nurse. Each sensation, each inclination to seek the renewal of a gratification once felt, he must take at first, at least relatively, in or for itself and at its face value. Until the necessity is felt for the subordination of some impulses, and the emphasis of others (those which are necessary for reproduction), as entitled to a relative primacy, the infant's tendencies might be compared to a set of loose threads of differently colored worsteds, lying side by side or crossing each other more or less at random, but not yet woven into a chosen, much less a beautiful pattern. The accomplishment of this latter task would mean health.

Nervous illnesses and faults of character thus arise largely as the primary or secondary results of the failure of the forces of civilization, as brought to bear on this or that individual child, to set the intricate machinery in action which should weave his threads into a good pattern. We need not now inquire where the fault lies; the main question is as to the effect. Let it be assumed that some special sort of gratification is too strong to be lightly abandoned in the child's mind in favor of the sort of subordination and co-operation offered by the oncoming years; or, to make the facts and argument seem more familiar, let it be assumed that the individual is drawn by some instinct to remain a child, with a child's egotism, longings, whims, propensities and a child's world of dreams and fancies.

I hardly know, though I might guess, how strongly this audience feels sympathetic to these Freudian doctrines. I do know, however, how I once felt myself. I well remember my own first attempt and failure — perhaps fifteen years ago — to grasp the real thought of Sigmund Freud, then a little-known physician, now deserving to be ranked as a great leader, and honored as we honor such men as Charcot, Hughlings Jackson and Pierre Janet.

I was glancing over a copy of the *Neurologisches Centralblatt* at a friend's house, when my eye was attracted by a bold claim concerning an asserted common origin for all the psychoneuroses. The paragraph stated that these neuroses never arose except on the [partial] basis of some disturbance of the sexual life and that the differences in the character of the symptoms, as, for example, between hysteria and neurasthenia, were determined largely by the period of life at which this or that disorder of the sexual life set in. I was impressed by the boldness and confidence of the statements, but rashly attributed these qualities to eccentricity and perhaps notoriety-seeking on the part of the writer, and laid the paper down with a distinct feeling of disgust: the reasoning, I thought, could not be correct.

How different are my sentiments at present, now that through three years' hard work I have learned what these statements really mean; have made the personal acquaintance of the author of them and his supporters, and have discovered what a treasure-house of facts respecting the deep currents of human life they have amassed. I have come to believe that if we had the power and the will to turn inward the searchlight of self-knowledge on a large scale, there would be far less prejudice and cruelty in the world than there is at present; far less envy, jealousy and suspicion; far less terror, disappointment, depression of spirits and suicide; far less disorders of the nervous system; far less inability to realize our best destinies. The whole great drama of life is played — in embryo as one might say — within the mind and heart of each and every individual, before he sees it played, — for the first time as he thinks, — on the larger stage of social world around him; and this fact is worth our knowing.

To bring about an advance in these directions, an advance in the prophylactic education of the child, an advance in the better understanding and treatment of neurotic invalids, would be well worth all the vast labor expended, or to be expended, on these investigations. It is not for the purpose of humbling ourselves that we need to scrutinize our repressed thoughts. There is little need of judgment but much need of freeing ourselves through wider knowledge from the unseen chains that restrain the utilization of the will.

We do not even need, in Oriental fashion, to forget. Every experience, if properly assimilated, may be made a stepping-stone towards higher things.

Printed by Libri Plureos GmbH in Hamburg, Germany